Today's a great day!

Some simple affirmations for nervous (and not so nervous) people

Larry Vazeos

Inner Peace Press
Eau Claire, Wisconsin, USA
www.innerpeacepress.com

For my mom and my sister, and Heather and Andy and Roger and Drew, Debbie, Angelo and Jimmy, my dad, Rob and Scott, Kyle & Kellan, Josh and Ellen, Franny and Tim, Deborah and Rody, Gavin, Liz and Laurie, Johnny and Dee, Tommy and Joey too, the gang at WJM, and mostly my grandma and grandpa.

Today's a great day! Some simple affirmations for nervous (and not so nervous) people

ISBN: 978-1-7351738-2-5
Published by Inner Peace Press

Images and text by Larry Vazeos

Let's start by acknowledging what's obvious to me beyond my unwavering love of ravioli and the color orange and that is that I am a work in progress and that if I live to be a 100 (which I intend to do) I'll continue being a work in progress, and by work in progress I mean that I am constantly evolving and generally moving forward. Of this I am pretty certain. Another thing I'm pretty certain of, after careful research, is that things in my life just keep falling in place as long as I let them.

Using simple positive affirmations is one of the tools that have helped me 'let things fall into place' and because they've helped me I wanna guess that they can probably help you, too. This book was created simply to inspire and encourage you to try and change the negative thoughts you might be carrying around in your mind about who you are. Without meaning to sound conceited, I've accepted that I am a much more delightful person

than I've allowed myself to believe I was in the past and I'm pretty sure you are too, so why not give affirmations a try?

I started (unintentionally) saying affirmations super early on. Many of the affirmations were negative: "I'm lazy," "I'm selfish," "I'm bad, weak, stupid, an inconvenience..." These were messages I heard. I adopted and believed them beyond the conscious part of my mind. I think I believed them deep in my mind, in my unconscious mind. They drove the truck and they steered the ship in my life for a long time. They were extremely powerful and acted in strong opposition to who and what I really was.

I was a good student but that didn't stop me from believing I was stupid. I knew I cared very much about people, yet I accepted that I was selfish.

I was surrounded by people who loved me, but I believed everyone hated me. These beliefs kept growing inside me.

For most of my life I've felt like I was making a mistake no matter what it was I was doing. I remember stepping off a curb once to cross a street and inside my head a voice said, "*that's* how you step off a curb?" I've very often felt 'in the way' or that I was an inconvenience just by being present or having this constant feeling of being a disappointment to whomever I was around.

Simple, positive affirmations have helped ease the anxiety that's almost always present in me. I wish I had more of these kinds of things to tell myself when I was a kid. Life might have been less stressful and painful. I probably would have enjoyed things more.

Before I started using affirmations intentionally, I could only control my nervous energy and fears by getting high one way or another – by numbing out or by just letting things slide hoping they'd just go away. I'd let others make my decisions for me because I thought I was incapable of making decisions myself and so I'd wind up even unhappier with myself and blaming everyone else.

Although I got turned on to affirmations a long time ago, they didn't become a more conscious thing I did until seven or eight years ago when I was back living in New York City. It was a really difficult period of my life. I was really scared and broke and really unhappy in general. I had this constant feeling of loneliness and isolation that felt like it was killing me. Affirmations seemed like the right thing to do because my mind was shot at

that point and just wouldn't shut up the rotten and mean thoughts directed at me and everyone around me even though I would pray and meditate frequently (maybe the idea of doing the affirmations was the answer to all that praying and meditating).

I remember being on the train one day and, in my head, starting at one side of the car and working my way to the other side, destroying everyone in front of me based on what they looked like or what they were wearing and I started to really feel sick like I was in hell or something and I remember asking God to please help me stop hating everyone and then I thought, "no, God please help me stop hating me." In that moment I knew that *that* was the problem – I couldn't stop hating everyone else until I stopped hating myself. Shortly after that I started doing affirmations from the second I got

out of the house (sometimes it'd start in the shower), through my train ride (sometimes an hour or more), lasting until I got to my destination.

I immediately started seeing a difference in my attitude and in my life. It was subtle enough for me to recognize that I really was doing and feeling better. Overall, it's been slow climbing out of my misery, but it's worked continuously; consciously thinking better thoughts about myself has helped give me a better life and a better outlook. In some 12-step meetings they'll say in unison at the end of the meeting, "it works if you work it, so work it because you're worth it."

My strongest belief has always been that it's a beautiful world, so why not do what I can do to be in line with that and express it? By telling myself I'm a good guy or that I'm safe goes a long way in how I conduct myself in

the world. I've been drawing figures like in this book for years. When I put them together with my handwritten affirmations and showed them to a few people, I got the idea to make this book. Just for you. To give you also the courage to switch the lies your brain is telling you. To tell yourself over and over again just how great you are, and how life, and today, is just as great as you can imagine it to be!

I hope you enjoy this little book.

Larry Vazeos
Between FL and CA 2020-21

I am
a celebration
of life.

It's okay
to feel
vulnerable.

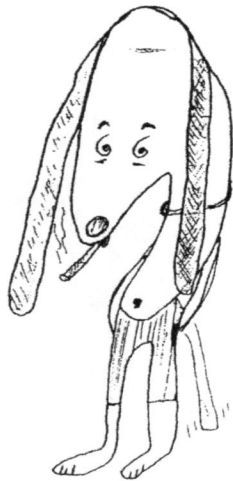

I am always on time

Affirmations help me counteract all the negative beliefs and thoughts I have programmed into my head about me and the world around me. They help me relax and they help me like myself in the moment — they make giving up or freaking out less of an option.

My life is fun and easy.

It's okay to feel sad.

I always have
time to
say hello

Level I

Myself

Affirmations help me get along better with other people — when I'm nervous or angry or afraid and it goes on for too long I tend to take it out on others — not always necessarily by my outward behavior but I've noticed affirmations calm the hostility I project with my mind, and I'd rather project love and kindness, which are really much more useful to everyone concerned.

I an allowed to shine.

I am accepting
of myself and
others.

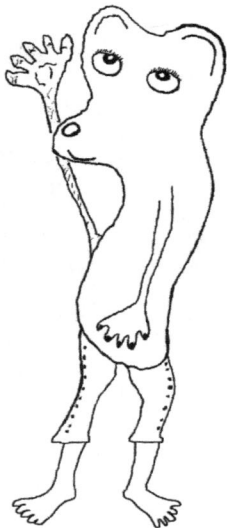

I am surrounded by kindness.

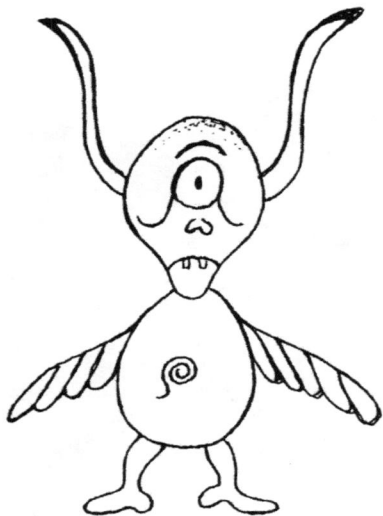

It's okay
to be
honest.

When do I use affirmations?

As soon as I wake up — I'm not taking any chances.
When I'm driving.
Before making a scary phonecall.
In any situation that scares me or when I feel nervous or angry or hopeless or down on myself.
Often.
Throughout the day — it really just takes a second or two to do sometimes and I figure that it's really just between me and me so there's no need to feel dumb about it.

I am
the breath
of God.

I have a
nice smile.

I am surrounded by love.

My essence
is sweet

This is the best
I can do today
and the best
I can do today is
good enough.

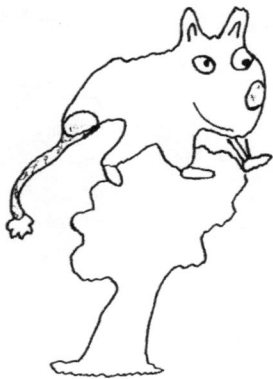

I am healthy.
I am happy.
I am terrific.

A long time ago a friend told me I had a bad attitude and it made me very angry. It made me angry because I knew it was true and because I knew I didn't wanna have a bad attitude and I especially didn't wanna hurt friends and hurt opportunities because of my bad attitude.

I just had to keep reminding myself that I have a good attitude.

I have a great attitude.

I am enjoying
the adventure of
what today has
in store for me

I have something special to offer everyone I meet.

It's ok
to be afraid

Affirmations help me feel more in control of my life, and I realize when I say them more often I'm a lot less scared and a lot more willing to just step out my door and try things.

I am
safe.

It's okay
to be nice.

Everything just keeps falling in place.

Affirmations helped me many years ago at a time when I was feeling really low and I desperately needed a job. There was a restaurant just around the corner from where I lived in L.A. and I decided I really wanted that job cause I so loved the idea of walking to work.

I started telling myself: "I'm the best waiter ever," "the manager loves me," "he thinks I'm perfect for the job," "they want me to start working there today," "everyone thinks I'm great," and on and on.

I suddenly found myself putting on my black pants and my white shirt (waiter's uniform) and I marched out of my apartment feeling like a million bucks.

I continued telling myself how much they loved me and what a great waiter I was non stop til I got to the door and through it.

The second I walked in, I caught the eye of the manager and he walked right up to me and said, "Can you come in tonight at 5 to start training?" and I said, "Thanks, I'll see you at 5."

I did it. I got the job. I swear I believe I created such an air of positivity around me that day that there was no way he could've responded to me in any other way.

I have good instincts

All my friends
think I'm great

I am allowed
to have fun

It's fun
to have fun

I am sane

About a year ago a guy asked me if I could draw a picture of this character from a movie called *Escape from New York* because he wanted to make a t-shirt and I said, "sure."

For almost ten years people have asked me to draw portraits or specific realistic things and I'd always say, "no, I don't know how to draw like that." But this time, because I really needed the money and couldn't afford to turn it down, I said, "of course I could" and I did and it turned out really cool....

... Now I don't believe that suddenly I was struck with the ability to draw realistically. I was able to do it all along, but for ten years I said, "no I can't draw like that." Reflecting on that is scary because it made me really wonder what else have I been telling myself I couldn't do that in actuality I could.

The difference was saying, "Yes, I can draw that."

It's time to have some fun.

It's okay to be silly

It's ok to be sensitive

Sometimes I say affirmations in the mirror. Especially if I'm in a rotten or negative mood — cause when I'm in that place my mind just wants to fight me.

I'll say, "I'm a great guy," and my mind'll say, "you suck," and I'll say, "I'm a great guy," and my mind says, "you stink," and on and on.

But, if I stick to "I'm a great guy," or increase it to "I'm a really great guy," or "I'm awesome," it seems to convince my negative mind to shut off.

The universe supports me in all my endeavors.

Today's
a great day!

I am appreciated
and adored.

My mind
and my body
are strong.

I use affirmations to help myself have a better attitude and to feel better about myself and to give myself a chance at a really good life filled with meaning and friends and fun stuff.

I can take
care of myself

I always come
in peace.

Be vigilant.

One of the things I can do is tell myself, "I'm smart" and "I'm talented."

Shortchanging myself has only succeeded in shortchanging myself.

It's ok
to have
desires.

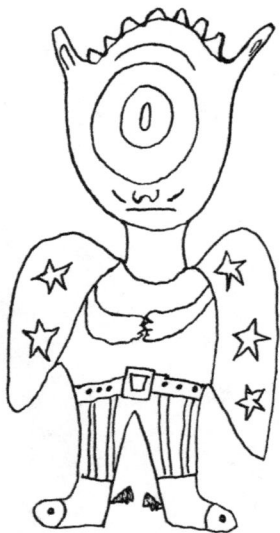

It feels great to be me.

It's okay to ask for help.

I'm finding that a positive mind is also very helpful for having an open mind. A positive mind invites more of the same. A positive mind is also energizing. Praying and meditating with a more positive mind invites in good ideas and visions.

I figure I'm gonna think no matter what, and although, obviously, I don't believe I can just sit here all day long repeating affirmations just like a Krishna devotee, I can use affirmations in the same way — to fill my brain with as much positivity and validation as I can. By doing so I'm gonna change "the habit patterns of my mind." (I learned this from Vipassana Meditation.)

I know affirmations work for me, and being no more special than anyone one else, I think others would benefit from using affirmations. It's a fairly simple principle: if I change my thinking I'm gonna change my experience.

I am smart.
I am talented.
I am every good
thing I can
think of.

I am surrounded by beauty

I am a worthwhile and lovable human being. I matter. I care about myself.

For many years I wrestled with the fear of spending money, even on ridiculous things like a bottle of water.

One day I found myself suddenly and automatically saying, "It's cool, I've got it. I ALWAYS HAVE PLENTY OF MONEY."

I said it like I meant it. I really did believe it at that moment and it wasn't connected to my bank account. It was connected to something greater — courage, confidence, whatever you want to call it.

It's not my lack or talent or creativity or intelligence that has stopped me, but a brain that repeats lies like: I don't have enough talent or I'm not smart or that other person is so much more creative than me so why bother or you'll only fail or make yourself look stupid.

These lies have thwarted the efforts of my life.

That realization lead me to affirmations. It was something I could do to get control of my brain.

I am a world class human being

I am loving.
I am kind.
I am good.

In the early days of my recovery from drug and alcohol addiction, I had this friend, Earl, who would wear these wooden beads around his wrist and I was intrigued by them, in my head I would refer to them as "Buddah beads."

One day I said to Earl, "Hey, do those help?" and Earl said, "Larry, everything helps."

So that's what I'm saying here: these affirmations help, they help me.

My affirmations work for me. Some of them might work for you. But really, it would be good if you write your OWN affirmations. See what you need and write down the words that will help stop your brain from telling you the lies it tells you.

Because it's like Earl said, "everything helps."

When you write your own affirmations it helps you to train yourself, like foster yourself, to allow yourself to just tell yourself good things about youself.

You can think of it like it's a game if that helps. Your mind plays games with you, so why not have some fun and play some tricks, too?

I am better
than good
I am wonderful.

It's ok to
be happy.

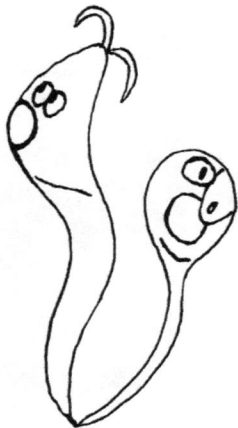

I like everybody

Larry Vazeos is a visual artist and a writer. He is left handed and has never had to wear glasses. His favorite color has mostly always been orange. He cares deeply and has many regrets. He has lots of friends of every variety and he wishes to say hello to all of them again some day. https://www.facebook.com/larryvazeos